NEW JEWISH TUNES.

AF001242

RUACH 5777
SONGBOOK

Editor
Joel Eglash

Executive Committee
**Cantor Rosalie Boxt
Joel Eglash
Dan Lange**

Review Committee
**Avital Abraham
Cantor Ben Ellerin
Molly Fidlow
Cantor Claire Franco
Alan Goodis
Danielle Rodnizki
Zoe Rosenberg**

includes audio download card

HEBREW PRONUNCIATION GUIDE

VOWELS
a as in *father*
ai as in *aisle* (= long *i* as in *island*)
e as in *bed*
ei as in *eight* (= long *a* as in *ace*)
i as in *pizza* (= long *e* as in *be*)
o as in *go*
u as in *lunar*
' = unstressed vowel close to ə
or unstressed short *e*

CONSONANTS
ch as in *Bach* or
Scottish *loch* (not as in *cheese*)
g = hard *g* as in *get* (not soft *g* as in *gem*)
tz = as in *boats*
h after a vowel is silent
r = like the Italian (rolled) or French *r*

No part of this book or recording may be reproduced in any manner without written permission from the publisher.

No sound recording featuring the works in this book may be made without proper mechanical license from an authorized licensing authority.

RUACH 5777: NEW JEWISH TUNES SONGBOOK
Copyright © 2017 Transcontinental Music Publications (ASCAP). All Rights Reserved.
Music engraved by Josh Wiczer – Copyedited by Debra Corman
Proofread by Cantor Ben Ellerin, Cantor Claire Franco, and Cantor Ross Wolman
Design by Joel Eglash – Cover design by Sara Streifel

Text material from *Mishkan T'filah: A Reform Siddur*,
Copyright © 2007, Central Conference of American Rabbis. All Rights Reserved.
Used by permission of Central Conference of American Rabbis. All Rights Reserved.
Not to be distributed, sold or copied without express written permission.

TRANSCONTINENTAL MUSIC PUBLICATIONS
A DIVISION OF THE AMERICAN CONFERENCE OF CANTORS
The world's leading publisher of Jewish music since 1938
1375 Remington Road, Suite M – Schaumburg, IL 60173
847.781.7800 – tmp@accantors.org
Printed in the United States of America – 10 9 8 7 6 5 4 3 2 1
ISBN 978-0-9976430-2-2

TranscontinentalMusic.com – NFTY.org
accantors.org – thegtm.org

Preface

RUACH IS THE HEBREW WORD FOR SPIRIT. It is exactly *that* quality which the songs of the *Ruach* series possess. These songs were chosen for their ear-catching melodies, for their colorful instrumental support, and for the life the music breathes into their texts. In short, all this is summed up by one common trait: *Ruach*.

The *Ruach* series is the continuation of the seven original NFTY (North American Federation of Temple Youth) albums that were recorded between 1972 and 1989. The NFTY and *Ruach* albums are primary sources of participatory music for camps, synagogues, schools, cantors, rabbis, educators, songleaders, musical leaders, and all those who disseminate Jewish music. Each *Ruach* collection reflects the spirit, energy, and vibrancy of the Judaism that lives and breathes in the camps, youth groups, and synagogues of Judaism.

Ruach 5777 represents a fresh, new start. It is the first *Ruach* published by Transcontinental Music under the supportive ownership of the American Conference of Cantors. In many ways, it is a return to the aforementioned, seminal NFTY albums of the 1970s: There is an intentional blend of acoustic group-vocal recordings next to fully produced rock and pop hits. In addition, we expanded our field, when calling for submissions, to not only North America, but to Europe and Israel. This yielded great results and will undoubtedly introduce you to new artists and sounds.

It remains for me to thank my fellow executive committee members, Cantor Rosalie Boxt and Dan Lange (representing NFTY and the URJ), who were instrumental in shaping this refreshing new direction for *Ruach*; our review committee members (great ears!); ACC president Cantor Steven Weiss and vice president Cantor Claire Franco; and the wonderful ACC/TMP staff: Rachel Roth and Stacey Berliner. In this, the ninth installment of this important series, we hope that you find new ideas and some earworms that will stay with you and your community, forever.

Joel Eglash
Founding Editor

Ruach is developed by Transcontinental Music Publications
in partnership with the North American Federation of Temple Youth (NFTY).

Thanks are due to the members of the *Ruach 5777* committees,
whose varying backgrounds and experiences helped shape
this remarkable collection of music, and, of course,
to the artists who have created this great music for all of us.

RUACH

The Ruach Series

Ruach 5761 and 5763 Songbook

Ruach 5765 Songbook
– Israel –

Ruach 5767 Songbook

Ruach 5769 Songbook

Ruach 5771 Songbook
– Social Action –

Ruach 5773 Songbook

Ruach 5775 Songbook
– NFTY's 75th anniversary –

5777

Adon Olam
Asha Sumroy and Ben Reiff 3

Asher Yatzar
Dan Nichols 6

Avinu Shebashamayim
Shimon Smith 8

Hal'li
Alan Goodis 10

Here I Am
Juval Porat 12

If Not Now
Sheldon Low 14

Modeh Ani
Michelle Citrin 16

Oseh Shalom
Becky Mann and Hooshir A Cappella ...19
SATB Choir Version 23

Shir Chadash
Jacob Spike Kraus 32

Sh'ma – You Shall Love
Shir Chadash at Am Shalom 33

V'ahavta
Daniel and Josh Warshawsky 35

Yih'yu L'ratzon
Elle Tzur 38

Artist Biographies 40
Ruach Series Indexes 44

RUACH 5777 SONGBOOK

ADON OLAM by Asha Sumroy and Ben Reiff
YOU ARE OUR ETERNAL GOD

Music: **Asha Sumroy and Ben Reiff**
Words: **Liturgy**

> We have always loved playing music together, and having grown up in the same youth movement, writing music has become a huge part of both our Jewish identities and our friendship. Even when we're not together, we send each other recordings of ideas we have—and that's actually how we wrote *Adon Olam*. For us, writing a more current and catchy tune for a piece of liturgy that is so commonly used to conclude our services was an important way to make prayer more accessible and relevant to the children we lead in our youth movement. It's been amazing to see it travel all over the world, through different branches of the movement, because for us the whole point of writing music is to share it.

Copyright © 2014 Asha Sumroy, Ben Reiff. All Rights Reserved.

Adon Olam (Asha Sumroy and Ben Reiff)

Adon Olam (Asha Sumroy and Ben Reiff)

You are our Eternal God,	אֲדוֹן עוֹלָם אֲשֶׁר מָלַךְ,
who reigned before any being had been created;	בְּטֶרֶם כָּל יְצִיר נִבְרָא.
when all was done according to Your will,	לְעֵת נַעֲשָׂה בְחֶפְצוֹ כֹּל,
then You were called Ruler.	אֲזַי מֶלֶךְ שְׁמוֹ נִקְרָא.
And after all ceases to be,	וְאַחֲרֵי כִּכְלוֹת הַכֹּל,
You alone will rule in majesty.	לְבַדּוֹ יִמְלוֹךְ נוֹרָא.
You have been, are yet,	וְהוּא הָיָה, וְהוּא הֹוֶה,
and will be in glory.	וְהוּא יִהְיֶה, בְּתִפְאָרָה.
And You are One;	וְהוּא אֶחָד וְאֵין שֵׁנִי,
none other can compare to or consort with You.	לְהַמְשִׁיל לוֹ לְהַחְבִּירָה.
You are without beginning, without end.	בְּלִי רֵאשִׁית בְּלִי תַכְלִית,
To You belong power and dominion.	וְלוֹ הָעֹז וְהַמִּשְׂרָה.
And You are my God, my living Redeemer,	וְהוּא אֵלִי וְחַי גֹּאֲלִי,
my Rock in times of trouble and distress.	וְצוּר חֶבְלִי בְּעֵת צָרָה.
You are my standard bearer and my refuge,	וְהוּא נִסִּי וּמָנוֹס לִי,
my benefactor when I call on You.	מְנָת כּוֹסִי בְּיוֹם אֶקְרָא.
Into Your hands I entrust my spirit,	בְּיָדוֹ אַפְקִיד רוּחִי,
when I sleep and when I wake,	בְּעֵת אִישַׁן וְאָעִירָה.
and with my spirit my body also;	וְעִם רוּחִי גְוִיָּתִי,
Adonai is with me and I shall not fear.	יְיָ לִי וְלֹא אִירָא.

ASHER YATZAR by Dan Nichols
GIVE US LIFE

Music: **Dan Nichols**
Words: **Morning Liturgy / Dan Nichols**

> I saw a cover of a magazine in the Whole Foods checkout line that said, "You're perfect the way you are . . . and you could use a little work." That stuck with me. Weeks later, while praying the *Asher Yatzar*, I felt there might be a meaningful connection to the wholeness and brokenness of being human.

Copyright © 2015 Little Nanny Dichols / Clashing Plaids (ASCAP). All Rights Reserved.

Asher Yatzar (Dan Nichols)

Blessed are You, Adonai,
who heals all flesh, working wondrously.

בָּרוּךְ אַתָּה, יְיָ,
רוֹפֵא כָל בָּשָׂר וּמַפְלִיא לַעֲשׂוֹת.

AVINU SHEBASHAMAYIM
BY SHIMON SMITH
PRAYER FOR THE STATE OF ISRAEL

Music: **Shimon Smith**
Words: **Shimon Smith (Based on the Prayer for Israel)**

> *Avinu Shebashamayim* is based on the Prayer for the State of Israel. The verses can be sung as a "repeat-after-me." Israel is my home and is open and available to all, not only as a place, but also as an idea. In this song we pray together for peace, understanding, and hope.

Na na nai nai nai, na na nai nai nai, na na nai nai nai, nai nai.

A-vi-nu she-ba-sha-ma-yim, A-vi-nu she-ba-sha-ma-yim, tzur Yis-ra-el, tzur Yis-ra-el v'-go-a-lo.

1. Wher-ev-er I
3. I pray for

1. go, wher-ev-er I roam, I al-ways know I have a home in Is-ra-el,
2. lost, I hope and pray, I know my heart will show the way to Is-ra-el,
3. peace, I pray for love, I pray that light will shine a-bove on Is-ra-el,

in Is-ra-el.
to Is-ra-el.
on Is-ra-el.

2. And if I'm A-

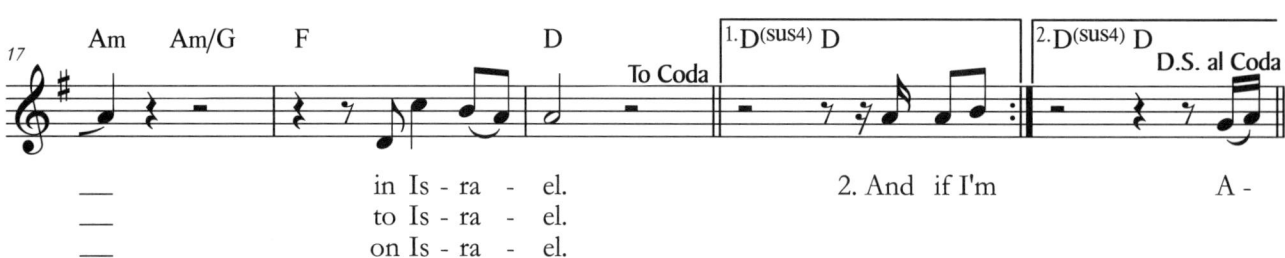

Copyright © Shimon Smith. All Rights Reserved.

Avinu Shebashamayim (Shimon Smith)

O heavenly One,
Protector and Redeemer of Israel.

אָבִינוּ שֶׁבַּשָּׁמַיִם,
צוּר יִשְׂרָאֵל וְגוֹאֲלוֹ.

HAL'LI  by Alan Goodis
PRAISE ADONAI

Music: **Alan Goodis**
Words: **Alan Goodis** / Psalm 146:1–2

> Psalm 146:1–2: *Singing and shouting praise to God for as long as we are living. When our soul is all that remains we will keep singing.* I came across this translation for Psalm 146 and immediately starting thinking about what my soul would sing when it *is* all that remains of me.

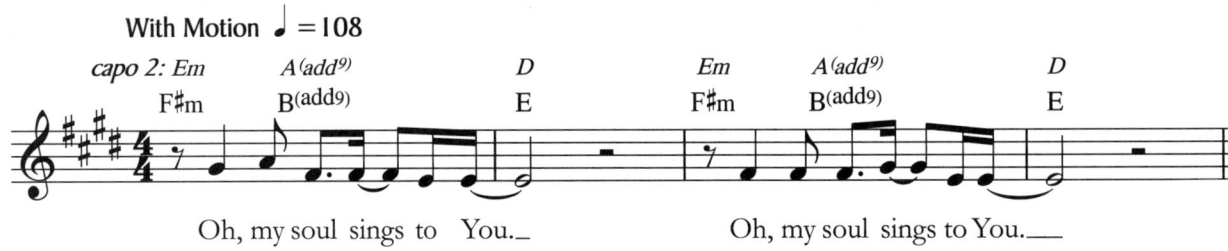

Copyright © 2010 O Goodis Industries Worldwide (BMI). All Rights Reserved.

Hal'li (Alan Goodis)

Praise Adonai, O my soul!
I will praise Adonai all my life, sing hymns to my God while I exist.

הַלְלִי נַפְשִׁי אֶת־יְיָ.
אֲהַלְלָה יְיָ בְּחַיָּי, אֲזַמְּרָה לֵאלֹהַי בְּעוֹדִי.

HERE I AM by Juval Porat

Music and Words: **Juval Porat and Tamara Kline**

> Most heroes today don't set out to be heroes. Rather, they see a problem or challenge at hand and think, "Something's got to be done here; I can help." *Here I Am* is a song that honors both the trepidation and the grace one often experiences when answering the call of *tikkun olam* with "*Hin'ni*, here I am."

Copyright © JAYPO-MUSIC, © PINK TRAX. All Rights Reserved.

Here I Am (Juval Porat)

Here I am. הִנֵּנִי.

IF NOT NOW BY SHELDON LOW

Music and Original Words: **Sheldon Low, Hadar Orshalimy**
Words Adapted From: **Amos 5:24** and *Pirkei Avot* **1:14**

"If Not Now" is the third line of Rabbi Hillel's quote, "If I am not for myself, who will be for me? But if I am only for myself, what am I? And if not now, when?" One of the consequences of living in a golden age for Judaism in North America is that we may take for granted the freedom and prosperity that those before us fought so hard to achieve. This song is a call to action, reminding us to get up and fight for justice and freedom not just for ourselves, but for all people, everywhere.

Copyright © 2016 Sheldon Low, Hadar Orshalimy. All Rights Reserved.

If Not Now (Sheldon Low)

Modeh Ani (Michelle Citrin)

Modeh Ani (Michelle Citrin)

I offer thanks to You,
ever-living Sovereign,
that You have restored my soul to me in mercy:
How great is Your trust.

מוֹדָה אֲנִי לְפָנֶיךָ,
מֶלֶךְ חַי וְקַיָּם,
שֶׁהֶחֱזַרְתָּ בִּי נִשְׁמָתִי בְּחֶמְלָה,
רַבָּה אֱמוּנָתֶךָ.

Oseh Shalom (Becky Mann and Hooshir A Cappella)

*May the One who makes peace in the high heavens
make peace for us and all the world.*

עֲשֶׂה שָׁלוֹם בִּמְרוֹמָיו,
סָלָאם עָלֵינוּ וְעַל כָּל הָעוֹלָם.

OSEH SHALOM BY BECKY MANN AND HOOSHIR A CAPPELLA

MAY THE ONE WHO MAKES PEACE

Music: **Becky Mann**
Words: **Becky Mann / Liturgy**
Excerpt from *Od Yavo Shalom (Salaam)*—Words and Music: **Mosh Ben Ari**

For Solo Voice and SATB Choir a cappella

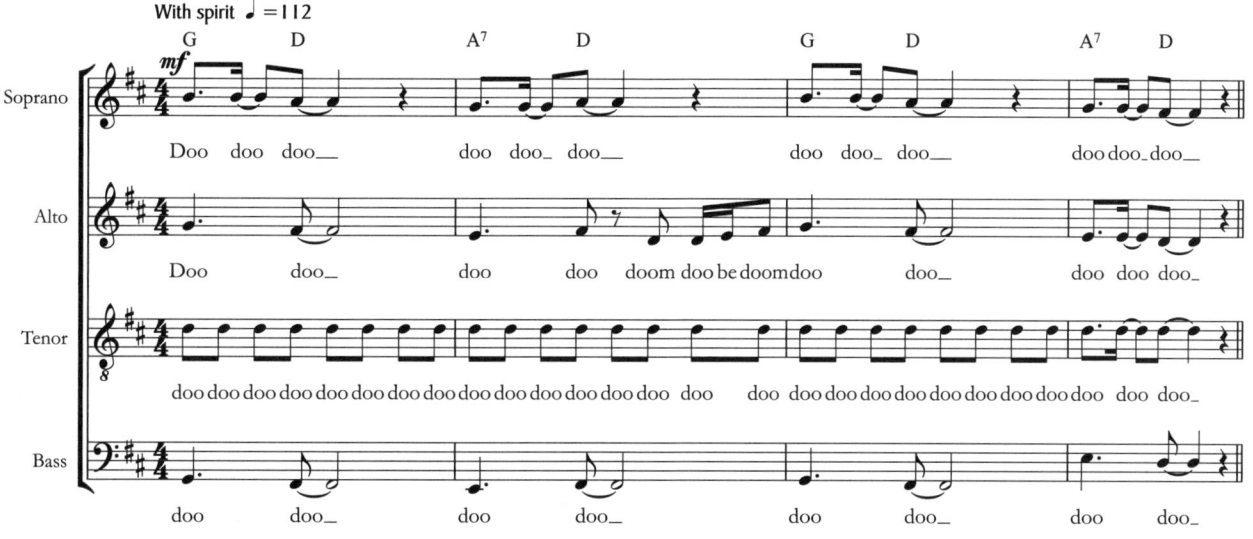

Copyright © Becky Mann. All Rights Reserved.
Od Yavo Shalom (Salaam) Copyright © Sheva (ACUM). All Rights Reserved.

Oseh Shalom (Becky Mann and Hooshir A Cappella) (SATB)

Oseh Shalom (Becky Mann and Hooshir A Cappella) (SATB)

Oseh Shalom (Becky Mann and Hooshir A Cappella) (SATB)

Oseh Shalom (Becky Mann and Hooshir A Cappella) (SATB)

Oseh Shalom (Becky Mann and Hooshir A Cappella) (SATB)

Oseh Shalom (Becky Mann and Hooshir A Cappella) (SATB)

SHIR CHADASH by JACOB SPIKE KRAUS
SING A NEW SONG

Music & English Lyrics: **Jacob Kraus**
Hebrew Lyrics: **Psalm 96:1–2**

The whole idea behind my album *Shake Off the Dust* was to reinvigorate Jewish music with a new energy and sound. The text of Psalm 96 perfectly fit that message of renewal: Sing a *new* song unto God. Writing a fresh new take on that particular text was a way I could encapsulate the whole message of the album in one song.

Sing to Adonai a new song,
sing to Adonai, all the earth.
Sing to Adonai, bless God's name,
proclaim God's victory day after day.

שִׁירוּ לַיְיָ שִׁיר חָדָשׁ,
שִׁירוּ לַיְיָ כָּל־הָאָרֶץ.
שִׁירוּ לַיְיָ, בָּרְכוּ שְׁמוֹ,
בַּשְּׂרוּ מִיּוֹם־לְיוֹם יְשׁוּעָתוֹ.

Copyright © 2015 by the Composer. All rights reserved.

SH'MA - YOU SHALL LOVE

BY SHIR CHADASH AT AM SHALOM

Music: **Sam Powers, Zach Powers, Meryl Rudy**
Words: **Liturgy / Shir Chadash at Am Shalom**

> On February 21, 2016, the members of Am Shalom's teen band, Shir Chadash (Alex Gordon, Sam Powers, Zach Powers, Meryl Rudy, David Sommer, Matt Sosler, Zoe Wilhelmsen, and Samantha Wolfberg) and Cantor Andrea Rae Markowicz met for a jam session after religious school. Sam, Zach, and Meryl introduced a melody they wrote with the intention of setting it to a prayer. The group decided on the *Sh'ma* and furthermore to write their own interpretation, in English, of the *V'ahavta* prayer.

Copyright © 2016 Sam Powers, Zach Powers, Meryl Rudy. All Rights Reserved.

Sh'ma – You Shall Love (Shir Chadash at Am Shalom)

Hear, O Israel, Adonai is our God, Adonai is One!
Blessed is God's glorious majesty forever and ever.

שְׁמַע יִשְׂרָאֵל יְיָ אֱלֹהֵינוּ יְיָ אֶחָד.
בָּרוּךְ שֵׁם כְּבוֹד מַלְכוּתוֹ לְעוֹלָם וָעֶד.

V'ahavta (Daniel and Josh Warshawsky)

V'ahavta (Daniel and Josh Warshawsky)

Love your neighbor as yourself.

If I am not for myself, who will be for me?

With all your heart, with all your soul, and with all your might.

וְאָהַבְתָּ לְרֵעֲךָ כָּמוֹךָ.

אִם לֹא עַכְשָׁיו, אֵימָתַי?

בְּכָל־לְבָבְךָ וְנַפְשְׁךָ מְאֹדֶךָ.

YIH'YU L'RATZON
MAY THE WORDS OF MY MOUTH

BY ELLE TZUR FEAT. LISA SILVERSTEIN TZUR

Music: Elle Tzur
Words: Psalm 19:15

> I was raised in a household that deeply enjoyed Jewish music, and our soundtrack included many Jewish artists who visited our home congregation on a regular basis. When I started to write Jewish music myself, I set out to honor the musicians that I had grown to love, but to also create something fresh, new and exciting for my generation. I think that every generation finds it own way to lift its prayer to a new level of holiness, and I feel honored to be part of a community that embraces that idea.

Copyright © 2017 Danielle Michal Tzur. All Rights Reserved.

Yih'yu L'ratzon (Elle Tzur)

May the words of my mouth and the meditations of my heart
be acceptable to You, Adonai, my Rock and my Redeemer.

יִהְיוּ לְרָצוֹן אִמְרֵי פִי וְהֶגְיוֹן לִבִּי
לְפָנֶיךָ, יְיָ צוּרִי וְגוֹאֲלִי.

ARTIST BIOGRAPHIES

RUACH 5777 SONGBOOK

MICHELLE CITRIN is an award-winning Brooklyn-based singer/songwriter and producer whose music is celebrated in Jewish communities around the world. With YouTube viral video hits "20 Things to Do with Matzah," "Rosh Hashanah Girl," and "Call Your Zeyde" reaching millions of hits, the press calls Michelle a "YouTube sensation!" Inspired by Rav Kook's words "What is old make new, what is new make holy," Michelle sets out to find connection points to our tradition's wisdom and culture in an easily accessible way, both on and off the *bimah*. Recently, Michelle was listed on Time.com's list of top 10 Jewish rock stars, and the *Jerusalem Post* calls Michelle "the Jewish IT girl." Visit michellecitrin.com.

ALAN GOODIS is a touring Jewish musician, playing over 150 events a year. Born and raised in Toronto, Alan is a proud product of URJ Goldman Union Camp Institute. Noted for his dedication to building relationships and community through music, Alan tours throughout the United States to serve as an artist-in-residence and performer at synagogues, youth conventions, and Jewish summer camps. In 2009, Alan's self-titled debut album, with its powerful vocals and bold melodies, launched him onto the Jewish music scene. Alan is a strong presence in the Reform Jewish Movement, engaging and empowering Jewish youth and adults through music. He's served as musical director for NFTY International Convention and on faculty at Hava Nashira. In 2011, he developed Nashir: A NFTY Teen Songleading Institute in partnership with the URJ. Alan has been a featured performer and presenter at URJ Biennials and the Wexner Foundation. In 2014, Alan released his album *This Place*. In 2016, Alan was named to the Chicago Jewish 36 Under 36. He lives in Chicago with his wife Codi. To learn more about Alan, visit alangoodis.com.

JACOB "SPIKE" KRAUS is an up-and-coming singer-songwriter from Boston. He released his first secular studio EP, *The King's Beanie EP*, and is currently touring his first full-length studio album, *Shake Off the Dust*, released in 2015. Based out of Astoria, New York, Jacob is the youth advisor at Temple Sinai of Roslyn, where he also serves as a music teacher. He has been songleading for over a decade at synagogues, schools, and summer camps, having served as head songleader at both the URJ Eisner Camp and the URJ Kutz Camp, for several summers. He graduated from Muhlenberg College in the spring of 2013 with a degree in music performance. A member of the Jewish a cappella group Six13, JSK believes in music's power as a community builder. He tours the country singing with communities and using Jewish music as a tool to educate and engage the next generation of Jews. Find out more about Jacob and his music at jacobspikekraus.com.

ARTIST BIOGRAPHIES

SHELDON LOW continues to establish himself as one of the most prominent and consistently relevant voices in contemporary Jewish music, having just released his fifth studio album, *Life*. The first single, *Shehecheyanu (To Life)*, was selected as the opening track for *Ruach 5775*, giving Low the distinction of being the only artist with opening tracks on two *Ruach* albums. A self-proclaimed road warrior, Low performs in over 100 concerts, services, and workshops each year. In addition to becoming a mainstay of congregational life, Low's music has become the soundtrack of the lives of hundreds of thousands of children around the globe, thanks in part to PJ Library distributing two of his children's albums and featuring him on countless other compilation albums. Beyond his acclaim as a Jewish musician and educator, Low is a highly regarded Jewish thought leader, leading seminars, webinars, and featured-speaking engagements around the country, and having served as a founding head faculty member of Songleader Boot Camp, as artist relations, social media, and blog manager for Jewish Rock Radio, and as a member of the Schusterman ROI network. Low is also a co-author of *Music: Carrier of Intention in 49 Jewish Prayers* (Creating Calm Network Publishing). Low is currently the artist-in-residence at Temple Israel of the City of New York and resides in Manhattan with his wife and musical partner, Hadar Orshalimy. Together they are known as the folk-pop duo We are the Northern Lights. Visit sheldonlow.com.

BECKY MANN is a senior at Indiana University, studying Jewish sacred music with a minor in general music. Born and raised in Las Vegas, she has served as the cantorial intern at Congregation Ner Tamid and the music specialist at Summit Ridge Day Camp. Becky is currently the alto one section leader of the Grammy-nominated Singing Hoosiers, the vocal director of a Bloomington children's show choir (Synchronicity), and the music director of Hooshir A Cappella. Her *Oseh Shalom* was awarded Best Original Arrangement at the 2014 Kol HaOlam National Jewish A Cappella Competition and was featured as a bonus track on the Cantors Assembly Spirit Series CD (Volume 13). When she isn't writing Jewish music, Becky enjoys writing comedic parodies and rapping the entire *Hamilton* soundtrack. More of Becky's original music can be found at soundcloud.com/user-283313390.

ARTIST BIOGRAPHIES

RUACH 5777 SONGBOOK

DAN NICHOLS is a product of the Jewish camping movement. He spent ten summers at the Goldman Union Camp in Zionsville, Indiana, before receiving his degree in vocal performance at the University of North Carolina. In 1995, Dan established the Jewish rock band Eighteen. Since that time, Dan and Eighteen have released ten full-length studio albums. His live performances are legendary for their unrestrained energy and infectious spirit. Dan spends more than 180 days each year on the road, where he often serves as artist-in-residence for congregations and camp communities. He has performed live in Israel at the historic fortress of Masada and in the studio for the groundbreaking XM Radio presentation of Radio Hanukkah. Dan created the Road to Eden Deep South Sukkot Tour and film to bring the music and message of Sukkot to numerous communities in the southern United States. Dan has been featured at conferences and conventions of nearly every major Jewish movement, including the URJ Biennial, NFTY Convention, BBYO International, and Limmud. Visit dannicholsmusic.com.

JUVAL PORAT, former architect and graduate of the Abraham Geiger College, is the first Reform cantor to be ordained in Germany after World War II. He has recorded two albums of original music and is looking forward to the completion of another. Juval currently serves congregation Beth Chayim Chadashim in Los Angeles, California. Co-writer **Tamara Kline** is an accomplished composer, producer, and arranger, who has written hundreds of television commercials and themes, including the main title theme for the CBS Winter Olympics in Albertville, Lillehammer, and Nagano. She is now a licensed marriage and family therapist in Beverly Hills, California, and a proud member of Temple Beth Chayim Chadashim in Los Angeles. Visit tktherapy.com.

SHIR CHADASH AT AM SHALOM is the post–b'nei mitzvah band, formed in 2014, at Am Shalom in Glencoe, Illinois. Under the direction of Cantor Andrea Rae Markowicz, the group plays at High Holy Days family services, various Shabbat services, religious school *t'filah,* and family concerts throughout the year. These young budding musicians of "Jew-sic," or Jewish music, act as religious school musical *madrichim,* accompanying the Ruach Children's Choir and visiting classrooms, and ultimately inspiring our community through Jewish music. For more information, please visit amshalom.com.

ARTIST BIOGRAPHIES

SHIMON SMITH is one of the leading Jewish-Israeli songleaders and performers in Israel. Shimon brings with him a combination of many different worlds: the new and old, rock and blues, Israeli, and American. His unique style of songleading brings a message of unity, community, and musical connection to Judaism and Israel. Shimon is the head songleader at Beit Daniel in Tel Aviv, tours as a bass singer with the Voca People, and tours summer camps. Visit shimonsmith.com.

BEN REIFF (right) is a student at the London School of Economics. He grew up in London and was active in the Reform Jewish youth movement RSY-Netzer, within which he developed a love and passion for Jewish music. **ASHA SUMROY** (left), also from London, is currently on her gap year in Israel, with the Reform Jewish youth movement RSY-Netzer. Music has always played a large part in her life and studies.

DANIELLE TZUR is a young musician and youth leader who attended her first NFTY convention at the age of four months. For Danielle, or Elle, music is a vehicle to bring her peers together, to create stronger communal bonds, and to communicate Jewish values. Her mother, **LISA TZUR**, found her Jewish calling through Jewish arts, particularly through contemporary Jewish music, dance, and yoga. Lisa explores the intersection of Jewish thought and healthful living, creating opportunities for connection in the Jewish community. Danielle and Lisa currently reside in the San Francisco Bay Area. Visit lisatzur.com and danielletzur.com.

ARTIST BIOGRAPHIES

JOSH WARSHAWSKY has shared his original melodies with Jewish communities throughout Israel, the United States, Canada, and the United Kingdom. In 2013, he released a five-song EP of original Jewish melodies. This was followed in 2015 by his first full-length album, *Mah Rabu*. *Mah Rabu* features such hits as the title track, *Kol B'Ramah*, and *V'ahavta*, which can be heard at Ramah and URJ summer camps as well as at NFTY and USY conventions across the country. Josh is spending the 2016–2017 year studying in Jerusalem as part of his second year of rabbinical school at the Ziegler School of Rabbinic Studies in Los Angeles. Josh spends his summers at Camp Ramah in Wisconsin and also travels to summer camps across the country, teaching and sharing music and *t'filah*. Visit joshwarshawsky.com. *V'ahavta* co-writer **Daniel Warshawsky** also grew up attending Camp Ramah in Wisconsin. After finishing degrees in communications and Jewish studies at Indiana University, Daniel made *aliyah* in 2016 and is currently serving in the Israel Defense Forces as a paratrooper.

RUACH COMPOSER INDEX

COMPOSER	TITLE	VOLUME
Aronson, Noah	*Echad*	5773
	Sing a Song of Men and Women / Mi Chamochah	5775
Aronson, Noah, Saul Kaye, Todd Herzog, Elana Jagoda, & Folk	*Walking In the Light / Mi Chamocha*	5775
Attie, Marsha	*Sha'alu Shalom*	5775
Beyer, Stacy	*Al Hanisim*	5767
	The Candle Blessing Project	5775
	Hodu L'Adonai	5765
Carlebach, Shlomo, Neshama Carlebach, & Josh Nelson	*Y'hi Shalom*	5775
Carlebach, Shlomo / Sheva	*Salaam (Sheva) / Ki Va Moed (Shlomo Carlebach)*	5761 and 5763
Chaiken, Max	*Eliyahu Hanavi*	5771
Chernick, Aviva & Chris Gartner	*Boi Kalah*	5773
Citrin, Michelle	*Jerusalem*	5771
	Modeh Ani	5777
	Someday	5769
	Yih'yu L'ratzon	5775
Dropkin, Steve	*Bayom Hahu*	5767
	Hodu L'Adonai	5761 and 5763
	Oseh Shalom	5761 and 5763

COMPOSER	TITLE	VOLUME
Steve Dropkin, *continued*	*War No More*	5765
	We All Stand Together	5761 and 5763
The Fools of Prophecy	*Fanan*	5765
Friedman, Debbie	*Devorah's Song*	5761 and 5763
	Light These Lights	5761 and 5763
	Sow In Tears, Reap In Joy	5767
Geffen, Aviv	*Ekdachim Shlufim*	5765
Gimbel, Jeremy & Shira Tirdof	*Salaam Achshav*	5771
Glaser, Sam	*Pitchu Li*	5769
Goodis, Alan	*Al Sh'losha D'varim*	5775
	Esah Einai	5771
	Hal'li	5777
Hadag Nachash	*Shirat HaSticker*	5765
Herzog, Todd	*Tree of Life*	5769
Herzog, Todd, Noah Aronson, Saul Kaye, Elana Jagoda, & Folk	*Walking In the Light / Mi Chamocha*	5775
Horowitz, Sue	*Hinei Mah Tov*	5767
The Israeli Mechina's Zimrat Yah	*Hallel L'Adonai B'chayai*	5767
Jaffa Road	*Ana El Na*	5773
Jagoda, Elana	*Oseh Shalom*	5771

RUACH COMPOSER INDEX

COMPOSER	TITLE	VOLUME
Jagoda, Elana, Todd Herzog, Noah Aronson, Saul Kaye, & Folk	Walking In the Light / Mi Chamocha	5775
James, Mark Aaron	Egypts To Leave	5767
Katz, Neal	Or Chadash	5765
Katz, Noam	Al Kein N'kaveh L'cha	5773
	Am Yisraeil Chai	5765
	Bar'chu / Roll Into Dark	5775
	Halleli	5761 and 5763
	Modeh Ani	5767
	Nachamu	5769
Kaye, Saul, Noah Aronson, Todd Herzog, Elana Jagoda, & Folk	Walking In the Light / Mi Chamocha	5775
Klepper, Jeff	Open Up Your Eyes	5761 and 5763
	Rabbi Ben Bag-Bag	5761 and 5763
Klepper, Jeff & Dan Freelander (Kol B'seder)	Shalom Rav	5775
Kline, Tamara & Juval Porat	Here I Am	5777
Komar, Eric	Ein Kamocha	5773
	Hatikvah - Don't Give Up the Hope	5767
	Justice, Justice	5769
Kraus, Jacob Spike	Shir Chadash	5777
Leader, Scott & Billy Tiep	Psalm 150	5769
Less, Naomi	Thank You	5773
The Levins	Daniel's Round	5771
Levy, Ross M.	The Call	5771
	Heiveinu Shalom Aleichem	5775
	Hinei Eil / Trust	5769
	T'filat Haderech / Never Walk Alone	5767
Lilien, Felicia	Raise Your Voice	5769
Low, Sheldon	If Not Now	5777
	On 1 Foot	5767
	Shehecheyanu (To Life)	5775
Mah Tovu	Eitz Chayim Hee	5761 and 5763
	Hillel's Song	5761 and 5763
	L'chu N'ran'nah	5767
Mann, Becky & Hooshir A Cappella	Oseh Shalom	5777
Maseng, Danny	Mah Tovu	5761 and 5763
Meltzer, Steve	Make It a Bridge	5771
Moss, David	Jerusalem	5775
Nelson, Jon & Yom Hadash	War No More	5771

COMPOSER	TITLE	VOLUME
Nelson, Josh	Ayzehu Chacham	5767
	Halleluyah (Live)	5773
	L'dor Vador	5769
	Mi Chamochah	5771
	Tzur Chayeinu	5769
	Yih'yu L'ratzon	5767
Nelson, Josh, Shlomo Carlebach, & Neshama Carlebach	Y'hi Shalom	5775
Nichols, Dan	All This Rain	5773
	Asher Yatzar	5777
	B'tzelem Elohim	5761 and 5763
	Esa Einai	5769
	Eternity Utters a Day	5775
	Hashkiveinu	5767
	Hoshiah	5771
	Kehilah Kedoshah	5761 and 5763
	L'dor Vador	5767
	L'takein (The Na Na Song)	5761 and 5763
	Mayim	5773
	My Heart Is In the East	5765
	Or Chadash	5769
	Pitchu Li	5761 and 5763
	Sweet as Honey	5771
Pauker, Mikey	Hinei Mah Tov (Eeoohh!)	5773
	Shalom Aleichem	5775
	Sim Shalom	5771
Porat, Juval & Tamara Kline	Here I Am	5777
Posner, Ari, Michael Smolash, & Julius Freudenthal	Ein Keiloheinu	5769
Rapoport, Jay	It Could Be Amazing	5771
	L'chadeish et Ha'yashan	5775
Recht, Rick	Al Shlosha	5761 and 5763
	Anachnu M'vorachim	5761 and 5763
	Halleluyah	5773
	Let It Be Me	5771
	The Hope	5765
	V'ahavta	5767
	Yihyeh Shalom	5761 and 5763
Reiff, Ben & Asha Sumroy	Adon Olam	5777
Rothman, Chana	Ayeka	5773
	We are One	5775
	We Can Rise	5769
Sababa	Beauty of the World	5773
	Birkat Shalom	5769

45

RUACH COMPOSER INDEX

COMPOSER	TITLE	VOLUME
Schachet-Briskin, Wally	Al Tifrosh	5761 and 5763
Schafer, Beth	A Way to Say Ah	5761 and 5763
	Children of Freedom	5761 and 5763
	In This House	5769
	Lev B'lev	5761 and 5763
	Love Multiplies	5767
	Working for Shalom	5765
Sheva	Ba BaAhavah	5765
Sheva / Shlomo Carlebach	Salaam / Ki Va Moed	5761 and 5763
Shir Chadash at Am Shalom	Sh'ma – You Shall Love	5777
Silver, Julie	Sim Shalom	5761 and 5763
Singer, Toby	Sim Shalom	5775
Six13	D'ror Yikra	5769
	Home	5767
Smilow, Peri	Ashrey	5761 and 5763
	Hineini	5771
	One Small Step	5767
Smith, Shimon	Avinu Shebashamayim	5777
Smolash, Michael, Ari Posner, & Julius Freudenthal	Ein Keiloheinu	5769
SoulAviv	L'chu N'ranena	5773
	Reach Our Hands Out	5771
Spiro, Hannah	Mi Chamocha	5773
Sumroy, Asha & Ben Reiff	Adon Olam	5777
Taubman, Craig	B'yado	5761 and 5763
	Halleluyah	5775
	Rise Up	5771
Tea Packs	Hatikvah	5765
Tedde, Celia	Can You Hear My Voice / Sh'ma	5775
Tiep, Billy & Scott Leader	Psalm 150	5769
Tirdof, Shira & Jeremy Gimbel	Salaam Achshav	5771
Tzur, Elle	Yih'yu L'ratzon	5777
Warshawsky, Josh & Daniel Warshawsky	V'ahavta	5777
Westermann, Alison	Adonai Tzuri V'goali	5773
Yom Hadash (also see Nelson, Jon)	Broken World	5765
	When We Were Young	5761 and 5763
Young, Natalie	Adonai S'fatai Tiftach	5771
Zive, Bryan & Kol Echad	Rock and Redeemer	5769

RUACH TITLE INDEX

COMPOSER	TITLE	VOLUME
Adon Olam	Asha Sumroy and Ben Reiff	5777
Adonai S'fatai Tiftach	Natalie Young	5771
Adonai Tzuri V'goali	Alison Westermann	5773
Al Hanisim	Stacy Beyer	5767
Al Kein N'kaveh L'cha	Noam Katz	5773
Al Shlosha	Rick Recht	5761 and 5763
Al Sh'losha D'varim	Alan Goodis	5775
Al Tifrosh	Wally Schachet-Briskin	5761 and 5763
All This Rain	Dan Nichols	5773
Am Yisraeil Chai	Noam Katz	5765
Ana El Na	Jaffa Road	5773
Anachnu M'vorachim	Rick Recht	5761 and 5763
Asher Yatzar	Dan Nichols	5777
Ashrey	Peri Smilow	5761 and 5763
Avinu Shebashamayim	Shimon Smith	5777
Ayeka	Chana Rothman	5773
Ayzehu Chacham	Josh Nelson	5767
Ba BaAhavah	Sheva	5765
Bar'chu / Roll Into Dark	Noam Katz	5775
Bayom Hahu	Steve Dropkin	5767
Beauty of the World	Sababa	5773
Birkat Shalom	Sababa	5769
Boi Kalah	Aviva Chernick and Chris Gartner	5773

RUACH TITLE INDEX

COMPOSER	TITLE	VOLUME
Broken World	Yom Hadash	5765
B'tzelem Elohim	Dan Nichols	5761 and 5763
B'yado	Craig Taubman	5761 and 5763
The Call	Ross M. Levy	5771
Can You Hear My Voice / Sh'ma	Celia Tedde	5775
The Candle Blessing Project	Stacy Beyer	5775
Children of Freedom	Beth Schafer	5761 and 5763
Daniel's Round	The Levins	5771
Devorah's Song	Debbie Friedman	5761 and 5763
D'ror Yikra	Six13	5769
Echad	Noah Aronson	5773
Egypts to Leave	Mark Aaron James	5767
Ein Kamocha	Eric Komar	5773
Ein Keiloheinu	Ari Posner, Michael Smolash, and Julius Freudenthal	5769
Eitz Chayim Hee	Mah Tovu	5761 and 5763
Ekdachim Shlufim	Aviv Geffen	5765
Eliyahu Hanavi	Max Chaiken	5771
Esa Einai	Alan Goodis	5771
	Dan Nichols	5769
Eternity Utters a Day	Dan Nichols	5775
Fanan	The Fools of Prophecy	5765
Hallel L'Adonai B'chayai	The Israeli Mechina's Zimrat Yah	5767
Hal'li	Alan Goodis	5777
Halleli	Noam Katz	5761 and 5763
Halleluyah	Rick Recht	5773
	Craig Taubman	5775
Halleluyah (Live)	Josh Nelson	5773
Hashkiveinu	Dan Nichols	5767
Hatikvah	Tea Packs	5765
Hatikvah - Don't Give Up the Hope	Eric Komar	5767
Heiveinu Shalom Aleichem	Ross M. Levy	5775
Here I Am	Juval Porat	5777
Hillel's Song	Mah Tovu	5761 and 5763
Hinei Eil / Trust	Ross M. Levy	5769
Hinei Mah Tov	Sue Horowitz	5767
Hinei Mah Tov (Eeoohh!)	Mikey Pauker	5773
Hineini	Peri Smilow	5771
Hodu LAdonai	Steve Dropkin	5761 and 5763
	Stacy Beyer	5765
Home	Six13	5767
The Hope	Rick Recht	5765
Hoshiah	Dan Nichols	5771
If Not Now	Sheldon Low	5777
In This House	Beth Schafer	5769
It Could Be Amazing	Jay Rapoport	5771
Jerusalem	Michelle Citrin	5771
	David Moss	5775
Justice, Justice	Eric Komar	5769
Kehilah Kedoshah	Dan Nichols	5761 and 5763
L'chadeish et Ha'yashan	Jay Rapoport	5775
L'chu N'ranena	SoulAviv	5773
L'chu N'ran'nah	Mah Tovu	5767
L'dor Vador	Dan Nichols	5767
	Josh Nelson	5769
Let It Be Me	Rick Recht	5771
Lev B'lev	Beth Schafer	5761 and 5763
Light These Lights	Debbie Friedman	5761 and 5763
Love Multiplies	Beth Schafer	5767
L'takein (The Na Na Song)	Dan Nichols	5761 and 5763
Mah Tovu	Danny Maseng	5761 and 5763
Make It a Bridge	Steve Meltzer	5771
Mayim	Dan Nichols	5773
Mi Chamocha	Hannah Spiro	5773
Mi Chamochah	Josh Nelson	5771
Modeh Ani	Michelle Citrin	5777
	Noam Katz	5767
My Heart Is In the East	Dan Nichols	5765
Nachamu	Noam Katz	5769
On 1 Foot	Sheldon Low	5767
One Small Step	Peri Smilow	5767
Open Up Your Eyes	Jeff Klepper	5761 and 5763
Or Chadash	Neal Katz	5765
	Dan Nichols	5769
Oseh Shalom	Steve Dropkin	5761 and 5763
	Elana Jagoda	5771
	Becky Mann	5777
Pitchu Li	Sam Glaser	5769
	Dan Nichols	5761 and 5763
Psalm 150	Scott Leader and Billy Tiep	5769
Rabbi Ben Bag-Bag	Jeff Klepper	5761 and 5763
Raise Your Voice	Felicia Lilien	5769
Reach Our Hands Out	SoulAviv	5771
Rise Up	Craig Taubman	5771
Rock and Redeemer	Bryan Zive and Kol Echad	5769
Salaam / Ki Va Moed	Sheva / Shlomo Carlebach	5761 and 5763
Salaam Achshav	Jeremy Gimbel and Shira Tirdof	5771
Sha'alu Shalom	Marsha Attie	5775

47

RUACH TITLE INDEX

COMPOSER	TITLE	VOLUME
Shalom Aleichem	*Mikey Pauker*	5775
Shalom Rav	*Jeff Klepper and Dan Freelander*	5775
Shehecheyanu (To Life)	*Sheldon Low*	5775
Shir Chadash	*Jacob Spike Kraus*	5777
Shirat HaSticker	*Hadag Nachash*	5765
Sim Shalom	*Julie Silver*	5761 and 5763
	Mikey Pauker	5771
	Toby Singer	5775
Sing a Song of Men and Women / Mi Chamochah	*Noah Aronson*	5775
Sh'ma – You Shall Love	*Shir Chadash at Am Shalom*	5777
Someday	*Michelle Citrin*	5769
Sow In Tears, Reap In Joy	*Debbie Friedman*	5767
Sweet as Honey	*Dan Nichols*	5771
T'filat Haderech / Never Walk Alone	*Ross M. Levy*	5767
Thank You	*Naomi Less*	5773
Tree of Life	*Todd Herzog*	5769
Tzur Chayeinu	*Josh Nelson*	5769
V'ahavta	*Rick Recht*	5767
	Daniel and Josh Warshawsky	5777
Walking In the Light / Mi Chamocha	*Folk, Saul Kaye, Noah Aronson, Todd Herzog, and Elana Jagoda*	5775
War No More	*Steve Dropkin*	5765
	Jon Nelson and Yom Hadash	5771
A Way to Say Ah	*Beth Schafer*	5761 and 5763
We All Stand Together	*Steve Dropkin*	5761 and 5763
We are One	*Chana Rothman*	5775
We Can Rise	*Chana Rothman*	5769
When We Were Young	*Yom Hadash*	5761 and 5763
Working for Shalom	*Beth Schafer*	5765
Y'hi Shalom	*Shlomo Carlebach, Neshama Carlebach, and Josh Nelson*	5775
Yihyeh Shalom	*Rick Recht*	5761 and 5763
Yih'yu L'ratzon	*Josh Nelson*	5767
	Michelle Citrin	5775
	Elle Tzur	5777